Explorers:
Triumphs and Troubles

Written by Paul Mason

Cover images: 123RF.com: Irina Tischenko; Shutterstock.com: Fedor Korolevskiy.

Acknowledgments: (Key: b-bottom; c-center; l-left; r-right; t-top) 123RF.com: Irina Tischenko 5cl, Sergii Denysov 4-5, Simone Gatterwe 4br, tribalium123 7, 11, 15, 19, 21, 25, 29, 30cl, 31tl; Alamy Images: Amazon-Images 18b, Blue Gum Pictures 29cr, Cephas Picture Library 9b, Classic Image 26tr, dieKleinert 17bl, Everett Collection Historical 30cr, Heritage Image Partnership Ltd 8t, Ivy Close Images 7bl, 13b, Mary Evans Picture Library 22cl, 24bl, 27br, National Geographic Image Collection 15bl, North Wind Picture Archives 13cl, 31tr, Russotwins 25b, The Keasbury-Gordon Photograph Archive 20bl, World History Archive 26t; Fotolia.com: Christos Georghiou 14br, 17cr, 18br, 22br, 26, didecs 3c, 4bl, 5c, 30, 31; Getty Images: Hulton Archive 11cr; Shutterstock.com: Alon Othnay 7tl, Fedor Korolevskiy 4tr, Ivaschenko Roman 5tr, 30br, Vadim Sadovski 24t.

ISBN-13: 978-0-328-85391-5
ISBN-10: 0-328-85391-7

16 22

Contents

EXPLORERS

Humans have always been explorers. Our earliest ancestors spread far and wide so that eventually people were living on every continent except Antarctica. The people who found these new lands were the first explorers.

Why Explore?

Explorers set off on their journeys for many different reasons:

Looking for Land

The first explorers were probably in search of new lands. As the number of humans on Earth grew, people began to look for new places to live.

Route Finding

Some explorers wanted to find a new route to a place they already knew about. Christopher Columbus, for example, was trying to find a new way to reach Asia when instead he stumbled across what we now call the Americas.

Hunting for Wealth

Exploring is often dangerous, and sometimes it's deadly. The risk may be worthwhile if you get rich, though! The Spanish explorers of the 1500s who searched for South America's legendary "Golden One," El Dorado, were examples of wealth seekers. They were looking to get rich.

Fame and Glory

Being the first to do something—climb Mount Everest or reach the South Pole, for example—meant you would be remembered in the history books. By the early 1900s many of these "firsts" were being checked off by fame-hungry explorers.

Between the 1400s and the 1800s, many explorers claimed to have discovered new lands, but these lands already had people living there. In fact, the locals had sometimes been living there for tens of thousands of years. How do you think they might have felt about being "discovered"?

Marco Polo and the Silk Road

Imagine being just seventeen years old and setting off for the other side of the world! Your dad (whom you only met two years ago) and your uncle are with you.

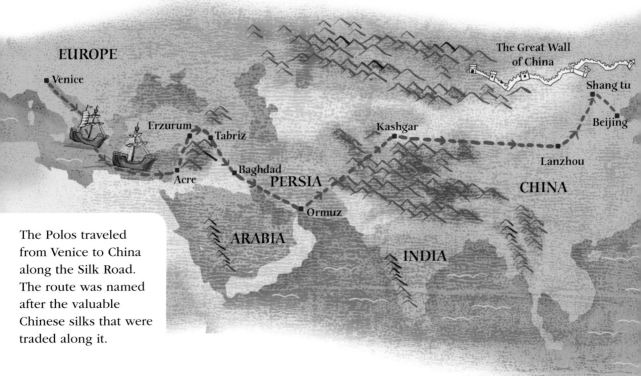

The Polos traveled from Venice to China along the Silk Road. The route was named after the valuable Chinese silks that were traded along it.

The Silk Road to China

That seventeen-year-old was Marco Polo, and the year was 1271. Marco Polo and his companions were setting out from Italy on the Silk Road, an ancient trade route between Europe and China. After many adventures, they finally reached the Chinese Emperor Kublai Khan's palace in about 1275.

Marco was a clever young man, and he eventually became Kublai Khan's advisor. Unlike other foreigners, Marco was allowed to travel throughout China. In fact, Kublai Khan found Marco's advice so useful that seventeen years passed before he was allowed to return home to Italy.

Marco Polo's book inspired traders to follow the Silk Road. The growth in trade brought wealth and new ideas to Europe, China, and the places in between.

The Travels of Marco Polo

When Marco Polo *did* get home, he found there was a war between his hometown of Venice and nearby Genoa. He was taken prisoner by the enemy. While he was in prison, he met a writer named Rustichello da Pisa. Da Pisa wrote a book of Marco's experiences called *The Travels of Marco Polo*. The book told readers about the people and customs of China, and it was a hit throughout Europe. As a result, Marco Polo became one of the world's most famous explorers.

Journey Fact File

Date: 1271–1295

Length of route: up to 6,200 miles (10,000 km)

Time for journey: over a year

Dangers: bandits, wild animals, desert sandstorms, cold and snow in the mountains, hunger and thirst

...or Trouble?

China was a secretive place, where foreigners were not allowed to travel freely. But *The Travels of Marco Polo* told people all about China and its customs. Imagine how the people of China would have felt if their enemies had used this knowledge to attack them.

Expedition to Tibet

In 1903, a British expedition to Tibet set out from India, which at the time was ruled by Britain. Little was known about Tibet, as foreigners had been banned since the 1850s. Francis Younghusband led the expedition. Younghusband was not only an explorer, he was also an officer in the British Army—and he took 3,000 soldiers with him.

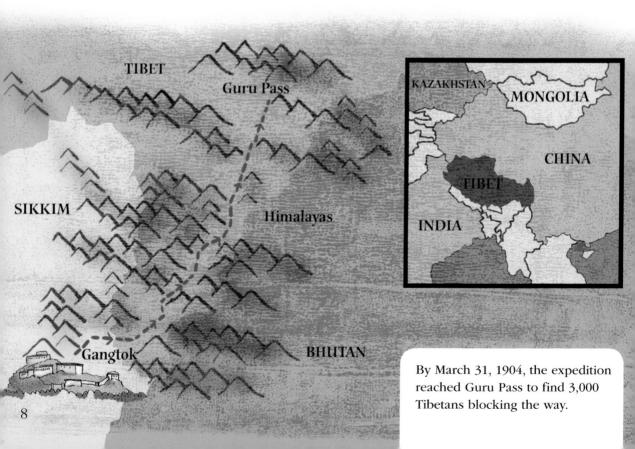

By March 31, 1904, the expedition reached Guru Pass to find 3,000 Tibetans blocking the way.

Reasons for the Expedition

Officially, Younghusband was going to Tibet to discuss a trade agreement between British India and Tibet, and to explore the country. However, there was another reason for his journey. British authorities in India thought Russia wanted to control Tibet. The British thought Russia was sending weapons to Tibet that could be used to stage an attack on British India.

Journey Fact File

Date: 1903–1904

Distance: 223 miles (359 km) in a straight line from Gangtok to Lhasa; much farther on foot

Numbers: about 10,000 people, including 3,000 soldiers

Dangers: attack by Tibetan forces, freezing temperatures, snow and ice, altitude sickness

Explorers Become Invaders

The Tibetans did not want the British Army in their country. They saw the British expedition as an invasion, which was what it soon became. To stop the British, Tibetan forces tried to block the road to the capital Lhasa, but the Tibetans were armed with old-fashioned weapons. Instead of turning back, as peaceful explorers would have done, the British Army opened fire with guns. The conflict was not balanced—hundreds of Tibetans were killed, but very few British soldiers died.

Scorched Earth

The Tibetans began to realize that they could not fight off the British and their powerful weapons. Instead, they began a "scorched earth" campaign where they destroyed anything the British might find useful. Villages were deserted, supplies were carried away and hidden, and crops were burned. The Tibetans thought that with nothing to eat, the British would go away. But this was not successful. The British had brought supplies with them, and they were able to fish in Tibet's lakes and hunt wild animals.

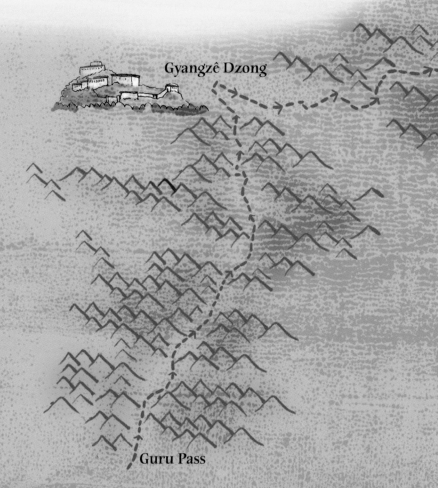

Gyangzê Dzong

Guru Pass

Lhasa

Triumph...

Leading the expedition across icy plains and through high mountain passes showed great leadership skills. And Younghusband was a patriot, trying to keep British India safe. He showed the Tibetans that siding with Russia was a bad idea.

A Trade Agreement

The British finally reached the Tibetan capital Lhasa on August 3, 1904, by which time all the Tibetan leaders had fled in fear. Younghusband forced junior Tibetan officials to sign an agreement that said the British could trade in Tibet. It also said Tibet had to pay reparations to make up for attacking the expedition. Until they were paid, the British would occupy part of Tibet's territory.

... or Trouble?

The Russian plan to control Tibet never existed, so the expedition was pointless. Even at the time, Younghusband was criticized for using powerful weapons against untrained, poorly armed Tibetans. Buildings were torn down, crops ruined, and part of the country was occupied.

11

THE AMERICAS

Cortés and the Aztecs

In 1504, at the age of eighteen, Hernán Cortés traveled to the "New World" from Spain.

Like many Spaniards who went to the New World, Cortés was a conquistador. This word comes from the Spanish word for *conqueror*. The conquistadors did not aim to become peaceful farmers. They went to find riches, and they weren't afraid to fight for them. These riches were sometimes gold or silver, or valuable lands, which they took from the people they conquered.

The conquistadors quickly took over the largest Caribbean islands, killing or enslaving local people. Their next step was to take over the mainland of Mexico.

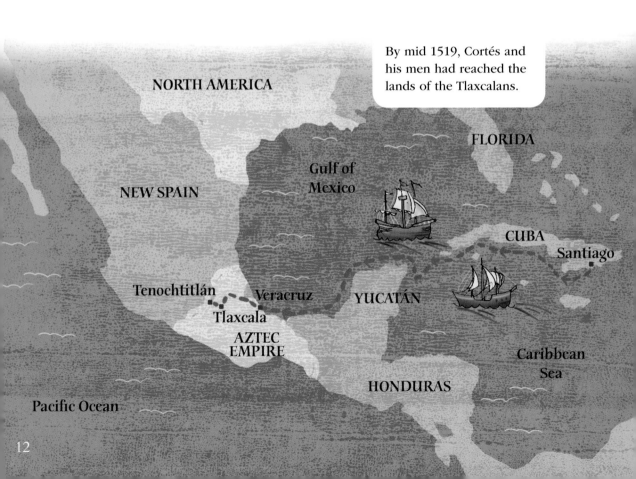

By mid 1519, Cortés and his men had reached the lands of the Tlaxcalans.

NORTH AMERICA

FLORIDA

Gulf of Mexico

NEW SPAIN

CUBA

Santiago

Tenochtitlán

Veracruz

YUCATÁN

Tlaxcala

AZTEC EMPIRE

Caribbean Sea

HONDURAS

Pacific Ocean

Cortés on the Mainland

In 1519, Cortés led the first conquistador expedition to Mexico in search of riches. With him were about 600 well-armed Spaniards. Cortés soon heard stories about the huge, powerful Aztec Empire. The Aztec temples were said to be full of gold. On hearing this, Cortés decided to head for Tenochtitlán, the Aztec capital city, to find his fortune.

Taking Sides

On their journey to Tenochtitlán, the conquistadors fought battles with the people whose lands they were crossing. Among them were the Tlaxcalans, who fought very hard and almost defeated the conquistadors. However, the Tlaxcalan leaders then decided to join the Spanish conquistadors. Together they made a large and powerful army to fight the Aztecs.

Cortés Reaches Tenochtitlán

When the joined forces of the conquistadors and the Tlaxcalans reached Tenochtitlán, the Aztec emperor Montezuma was not eager to meet them. He sent them gifts of gold, hoping this would make the Spanish go away. But the sight of gold only made the conquistadors more determined to gain riches. Finally, Montezuma could no longer hold the Spanish back, so he welcomed them to Tenochtitlán.

Badly Behaved Guests

Cortés was technically Montezuma's guest—but he was a very badly behaved one. He soon took Montezuma prisoner. This was a normal tactic for conquistadors, who often captured local leaders and then forced them to rule as they wanted.

NEW SPAIN

Tenochtitlán

Cortés had to leave Tenochtitlán in April 1520 to fight off a rival group of conquistadors who also wanted to rule Tenochtitlán. While he was gone, a member of his army killed a large group of Aztec nobles. This caused the Aztecs to fight back, and the conquistadors had to flee.

Should Cortés have attacked the Aztec Empire?

The Aztecs built their empire by attacking and conquering other people. So was Cortés only doing to the Aztecs what they had done to others?

The Capture of Tenochtitlán

After fleeing, the conquistadors and the Tlaxcalans soon returned. They surrounded Tenochtitlán, and in August 1521 it was captured from the Aztecs. The huge Aztec Empire became part of New Spain, and although many local rulers were left in place, the Spanish were in control. The gold, silver, and other wealth of the Aztecs now belonged to the Spanish.

Triumph . . .

Cortés was a bold adventurer and a great leader. The gold and silver he got from Mexico made Spain rich and powerful, and once they had conquered the Aztec Empire, the Spanish left many local rulers in place.

By August 1521, Cortés and his conquistadors had defeated the Aztec Empire.

Tlaxcala

AZTEC EMPIRE

. . . or Trouble?

Cortés was a ruthless, cruel man and was only interested in making himself rich. The Aztec Empire's wealth was taken back to Spain, leaving the local people with very little. Local leaders were controlled by the Spanish and could not make their own decisions.

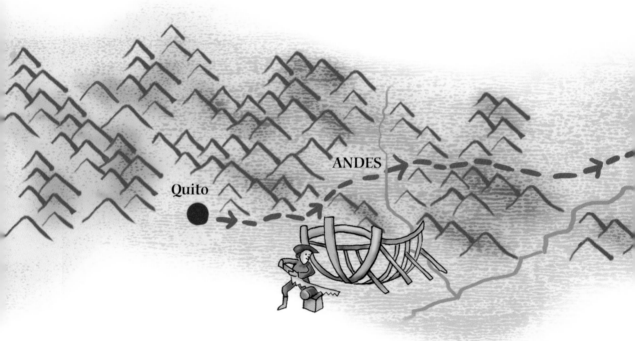

The Search for El Dorado

Almost as soon as they arrived in the New World, Spanish conquistadors became obsessed with a legendary figure named El Dorado, which is Spanish for "The Golden One." He was said to be a local ruler with almost limitless supplies of gold, and the conquistadors wanted to get their hands on it!

ANDES

Quito

Expedition from Quito

In 1541, a group of 200 conquistadors, along with about 4,000 local people and a variety of horses and dogs, set off to hunt for El Dorado. They left the city of Quito in what is now Ecuador in February and headed toward the Andes Mountains.

By December 1541, the explorers had crossed the Andes Mountains, but the expedition was rapidly running out of supplies.

After eighteen months, the explorers reached the Coca River. They had spent much of those months wandering around in the rain forest, trying to find information about the location of El Dorado. The conquistadors were now getting very hungry, and they badly needed help. Their leader, Gonzalo Pizarro, decided that they should build a boat. The boat would travel downstream, and the men would collect food and come back. Pizarro chose an officer named Francisco de Orellana to captain the boat. On December 26, 1541, Orellana and fifty-eight men set off to find help.

Coca

Coca River

What Do You Think?

Why did the conquistadors keep searching for El Dorado?

After leaving Quito, the conquistadors raided local villages for food, and they questioned the people living there to find out where El Dorado was. Might the villagers have realized that a good way to make the Spanish go away was to tell them El Dorado was far away from their villages?

Downstream to the Napo

At first, things did not go well for Orellana and his men—they got so hungry searching for food that they ate the boiled soles of their shoes! Finally, they found a village and food, but instead of going back to the rest of the expedition as Pizarro had instructed, Orellana and his men continued downriver away from the rest.

Journey Fact File

Date: 1541–1542

Distance to sea: 3,700 miles (6,000 km)

Time: 8 months

Dangers: starvation, sickness, attack by local people

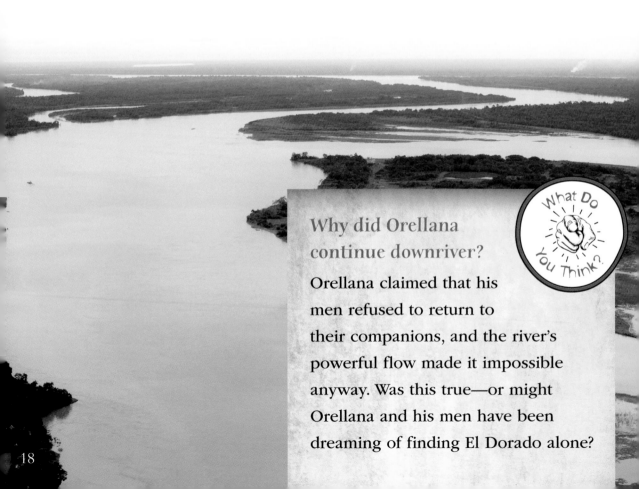

What Do You Think?

Why did Orellana continue downriver?

Orellana claimed that his men refused to return to their companions, and the river's powerful flow made it impossible anyway. Was this true—or might Orellana and his men have been dreaming of finding El Dorado alone?

Amazon Attack!

Eventually Orellana and his companions spilled out into a large river, which he named the *Río de Orellana*. A fierce band of what they thought were women then attacked the explorers. The attackers were probably men from the Yagua people wearing grass skirts, but the story reminded people of a mythical group of female warriors from Ancient Greece called *Amazons*. From then on, people started calling the river the Amazon, which is the name it still has today.

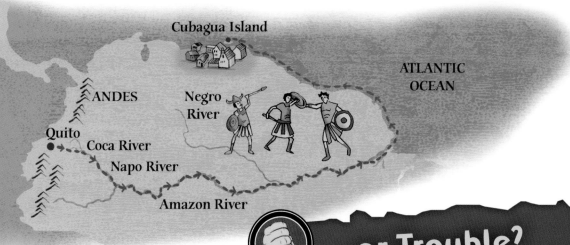

The Atlantic Ocean

Eventually, Orellana and his men reached the Atlantic Ocean. They turned north up the coast, and by September 11, 1542, they had reached the Spanish settlement on Cubagua Island, where they found safety.

ANTARCTICA

The Race to the Pole

In 1911, no explorer had ever reached the South Pole. That year, the British explorer Robert Scott announced his plan to go there at the same time as Norway's Roald Amundsen. It quickly became a race.

Preparing for the Pole

Scott prepared carefully for the journey. His team would use ponies and motorized sleds to carry supplies to "dumps" along the route, and the explorers would travel between these, collecting supplies as they went. After the last supply dump, they would "man-haul," which meant dragging their food and equipment along on sleds.

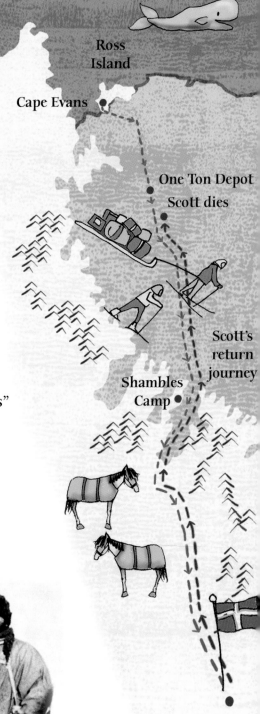

Ross Island

Cape Evans

One Ton Depot
Scott dies

Scott's return journey

Shambles Camp

SOUTH POLE

Scott's team set out for the South Pole from Cape Evans on November 1, 1911.

Bay of
Whales

Ross
Ice Shelf

Triumph . . .

Scott and his men made a heroic effort in terrible conditions. Even though their equipment did not work, they still managed to reach the Pole. In fact, some of them almost made it back.

Disastrous End

Scott's expedition was a disaster. The motorized sleds broke down, the ponies could not cope with the cold and ice, and man-hauling supplies was exhausting. Scott and four others reached the Pole five weeks after their Norwegian rivals, but they were too weak to get home safely, and all five of the explorers died.

Journey Fact File

Date: 1911–1912

Men in original party: 12

Route distance:
1,766 miles (2,842 km)

Time spent on ice:
5 months

Dangers: snowstorms, high winds, ice, subzero temperatures

←— Outward journey
-→ Return journey

. . . or Trouble?

Scott made a mistake. People already knew how to travel safely through icy wastes using dog sleds, skis, and thick furs, which had been keeping explorers safe in the Arctic for many years. Amundsen used these and succeeded, and Scott failed because he did not.

The First Fleet

On January 26, 1788, a group of Eora people
from Australia woke up to see eleven ships in
the bay where they lived. This was unusual,
as ships rarely passed through the bay.

England

Canary
Islands

ATLANTIC
OCEAN

Rio de Janiero

A Welcome Landfall

The people aboard the ships, which we now call the First
Fleet, must have been very pleased to arrive. Their journey
from Britain to Australia had taken 250 days, and they had
endured storms, shortages of food and water, and even a mutiny.

What Do
You Think?

Were the British right to claim Australia?

When the British arrived in Australia, they
decided that the land was legally *terra nullius*—Latin
for "no one's land." They thought this allowed them to
claim the territory for Britain. Do you think this was right?

The British Settlement

The new arrivals quickly began to put up tents and then to build roads, fences, and houses. Their settlement would have looked strange to the Eora, who lived, dressed, and used the land differently than Europeans. The Europeans thought they could come into Eora country and settle there, but the land belonged to the Eora.

Journey Fact File

Date: 1787–1788

Ships in fleet: 11

Passengers and crew: about 1,480

Time spent at sea: 8 months

Dangers: storms, shipwreck, fire aboard ship, sickness, thirst, hunger

Claiming Australia

The British knew before they arrived that people already lived in Australia, because another famous British explorer, Captain James Cook, had reached the coastline of eastern Australia in 1770 and made contact with the people who lived there. (We now call these people Aboriginal and Torres Strait Islander people.) However, the British also knew that there was no government, army, or police force, so they decided to claim the land as their own.

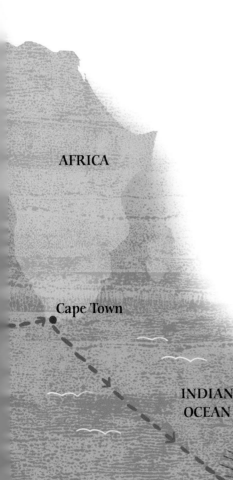

AFRICA

Cape Town

INDIAN OCEAN

AUSTRALIA

AUSTRALIA

Conflict Arises

At first the British and the Eora people did not fight, but soon they were in conflict. The Eora people had lived on the land for centuries and respected the land, taking only what they needed and managing it well. The British fenced off large areas of the Eora people's land, which prevented them from crossing it.

By 1790, many Eora were frustrated by the new arrivals. A local leader named Pemulwuy began a series of attacks against the British and became a great hero to many Eora. The conflict lasted until Pemulwuy was killed in 1802.

WANTED
Pemulwuy

CHARGED WITH:

The MURDER of John McEntire, the Governor's huntsman, and many other White Men

RAIDING and SETTING FIRE to the Government Farm at Toongabbie

Leading a HUNDRED WARRIORS into Parramatta Town

And other HEINOUS CRIMES too many to list

Triumph...

The arrival of the First Fleet was the start of European settlement in Australia. Since then, Australia has become a wealthy, modern nation. Its people are from European, Asian, and other backgrounds, and they all share in the country's success.

... or Trouble?

The arrival of the British was devastating for Aboriginal and Torres Strait Islander people. Two years after the British arrived, up to 70% of the Eora had died of smallpox. In the next hundred years, the total number of Indigenous Australians dropped from roughly one million to 60,000.

Today, Indigenous Australians make up about 3% of the population. For the most part they have not shared in Australia's modern wealth, and they are among the country's poorest people.

Burke and Wills

On August 20, 1860, crowds cheered as the Victorian Exploring Expedition left Royal Park in Melbourne, Australia. The explorers were aiming to make the first-ever crossing of Australia from south to north. Robert Burke and his second-in-command, William Wills, led the expedition.

Gulf of Carpentaria

AUSTRALIA

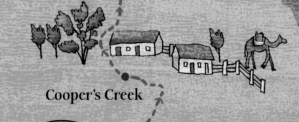

Cooper's Creek

What Do You Think?

Menindee

Melbourne

Was Burke the right leader?

Burke had been an officer in the Australian Army and the police, so he was a trained leader. He had no experience as an explorer, though, and Burke was famous for getting lost— even in his hometown!

Terrible Conditions

Conditions for the explorers were terrible. It was extremely hot in the day and freezing at night. Tiny black flies got in their noses, mouths, ears, and even their eyes. Rats nibbled the explorers' toes at night, and there were scorpions, venomous snakes, and mosquitoes. The expedition was also weighed down by more than twenty tons of equipment, including useless items such as a Chinese gong and a heavy dining table. The explorers struggled to cover 18 miles (30 km) per day.

Journey Fact File

Date: 1860–1861

Distance: roughly 2,020 miles (3,250 km) from coast to coast

Dangers: heat, cold, thirst, hunger, venomous animals

Number of explorers: 19 (more than 600 people applied to take part)

Weight of supplies: at first, about 20 tons

Transport: mainly camels (the expedition started with wagons, but these broke down on the first day)

Cooper's Creek

After three months, the exhausted explorers reached Cooper's Creek— not even halfway to the north coast. This was the traditional territory of the Yandruwandha people.

The explorers set up camp. They used as much of the creek's precious water as they liked, and they let their animals dirty the stream so that anyone farther down could not use it. But the Yandruwandha did not complain. They could see the explorers were exhausted and needed to recover. The Yandruwandha even brought them gifts of fish and other food.

AUSTRALIA

On to the North Coast

After a month at Cooper's Creek, Burke set off for the north coast with William Wills, John King, and Charles Grey. The others were told to wait three months at Cooper's Creek for their return.

By February 1861, the four men had gotten within 3 miles (5 km) of the north coast. Mangrove swamps blocked their way, and they turned back. Grey, who was exhausted, died on the way home, and when the others finally stumbled into camp at Cooper's Creek, they found that the rest of the expedition had left that morning.

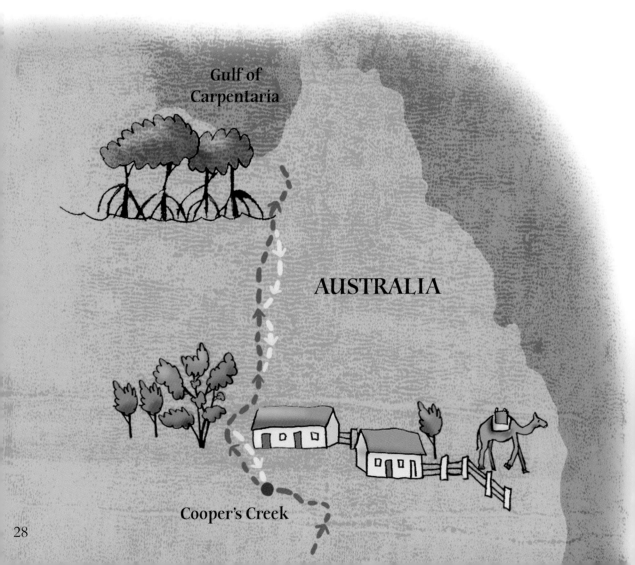

Gulf of
Carpentaria

AUSTRALIA

Cooper's Creek

The Deaths of Burke and Wills

The three remaining explorers now survived partly on food that had been buried by the rest of the expedition before they left. They had left instructions on a tree about where the supplies were buried. This is now known as the "dig tree." When the supplies ran low, the explorers were given food by the Yandruwandha. One day, Burke feared the Yandruwandha would steal expedition property, and he drove them off with a pistol shot. They did not return. Burke and Wills both died on about June 30, and the only survivor of the expedition was King, who was looked after by the Yandruwandha.

Triumph . . .

Burke, Wills, and King reached within 3 miles (5 km) of the north coast. If they had returned to Cooper's Creek just a few hours earlier, the rest of the expedition would still have been there and they would have made it back to Melbourne alive.

. . . or Trouble?

Burke put his ambition to make history ahead of the safety of his men. He also treated the Yandruwandha with contempt. He used water from Cooper's Creek, camped on their territory, and took their food—then shot at them. Even then, the Yandruwandha looked after King until the search party arrived.

EXPLORERS: TRIUMPHS OR TROUBLES?

Many explorers became heroes back at home—sometimes even if they failed! Scott of the Antarctic is a hero to many British people, despite reaching the South Pole after his rival and then dying with all his men on the way back. But were the explorers of the past *really* heroes?

Triumphs: Wealth

Exploration brought many countries great wealth. Spain, for example, became Europe's richest nation because of the treasure from its territories in the Americas. Each year, a "treasure fleet" brought gold, silver, jewels, pearls, and other valuables back to Spain.

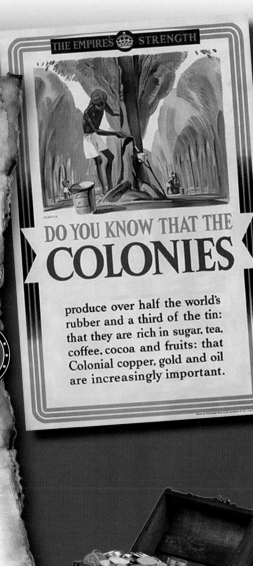

THE EMPIRE'S STRENGTH

DO YOU KNOW THAT THE
COLONIES

produce over half the world's rubber and a third of the tin: that they are rich in sugar, tea, coffee, cocoa and fruits: that Colonial copper, gold and oil are increasingly important.

Triumphs: Territory

Exploration allowed countries to expand their territory. Explorers paved the way for Britain to occupy lands in Africa, Asia, and Australia, for example. These new territories provided Britain with raw materials, such as rubber and oil, and they were also places to sell British goods.

Troubles: Land Thieves

The lands explorers found already belonged to other people. They occupied the lands without permission, often by force. Sometimes the explorers enslaved the local people, and the wealth they sent home was not theirs to take.

Troubles: Spreaders of Disease

Explorers often brought new diseases with them. Millions of people died as a result. In many places these diseases decimated the local population. To the people whose lands they reached, many explorers were definitely not heroes.

At the time, few explorers thought they were doing anything wrong. For example, they did not know their diseases would kill millions. But does that make it acceptable?

What do you think? Can we judge the triumphs and troubles of explorers based on things we know, but they did not?

Glossary

British India area of South Asia that was part of the British Empire
between 1858 and 1947

decimated greatly reduced or destroyed

massacre fight in which far more people are killed on one side
than on the other

mutiny refusal by ordinary sailors or soldiers to obey their officers

New World name given to North and South America by Europeans

occupied invaded and governed by the forces of another country

patriot person who is a strong supporter of his or her country

reparations payments made by one country to another, to make
up for attacking it in a war

smallpox infectious disease that has killed more people than any other

tactic plan to achieve a specific result

Index